ANIMAL
CONSERVATION

HARRIET BRUNDLE

PROTECTING OUR
PLANET

©2018
Book Life
King's Lynn
Norfolk PE30 4LS

ISBN: 978-1-78637-259-8

All rights reserved
Printed in Malaysia

Written by:
Harriet Brundle

Edited by:
Kirsty Holmes

Designed by:
Gareth Liddington

A catalogue record for this book
is available from the British Library.

Photocredits: Abbreviations: l-left, r-right, b-bottom, t-top, c-centre, m-middle. All images are courtesy of Shutterstock.com.

Covert – Josep Curto, Coverm – Hung Chung Chih, Coverb – dangdumrong, 1 – neelsky, 2 – JONATHON PLEDGER, 3 – Eric Isselee, 4 – Alena Brozova, 5 – Tatiana Volgutova, 6 – Alexandr Junek Imaging, 7 – AuntSpray, 8 – Allen Paul Photography, 9t – Boiarkina Marina, 9ml – Jesse Nguyen, 9mr – wawritto, 10 – Iakov Filimonov, Anan Kaewkhammul, Eric Isselee, Stefan Petru Andronache, Veniamin Kraskov, 12tl – yelantsevv, 12tr – BABYFRUITY, 12bl – Minerva Studio, 12br – nobeastsofierce, 13tl – Nickolay Khoroshkov, 13tr – Scharfsinn, 13mr – AlexLMX, 13bl – timotheos, 13br – Rich Carey, 14 – LesPalenik, 15 – nikkytok, 16 – IUCN (commons.wikimedia), DenisaPro, 17ml – Daniel Morales-Franchini, 17mr – Sharon Morris, 17m – JONATHAN PLEDGER, 18 – Elliotte Rusty Harold, 19 – Payton Chung (commons.wikimedia), 20 – Sergey Uryadnikov, 21t – Iakov Kalinin, 21b – Dmitry Polonskiy, 22 – Kohn Wollwerth, 23 – g-stockstudio, 24 – chris froome

Images are courtesy of Shutterstock.com. With thanks to Getty Images, Thinkstock Photo and iStockphoto.

CONTENTS

Words that look like **this** can be found in the glossary on page 24.

WHAT IS ANIMAL CONSERVATION?

To conserve something means to look after it and protect it from harm, damage or **destruction**. Each of us is responsible for helping to conserve our world.

A SQUIRREL'S HABITAT IS OFTEN A WOODLAND AREA.

Animal conservation is about the actions we can take to protect animals and the places where they live, which are called habitats.

ENDANGERED TO
EXTINCT

SIBERIAN TIGER

If we don't look after animals and their homes, the number of animals in a **species** could get smaller. If this happens, the animals are said to be endangered.

If a whole species of animal dies out, the species is said to be extinct. It is thought that thousands of species become extinct every year.

THE DODO BECAME EXTINCT IN 1662.

WHY IS ANIMAL CONSERVATION IMPORTANT?

Every animal and their habitat is part of an ecosystem. There can be lots of different habitats within the same ecosystem and they can each be home to different animals.

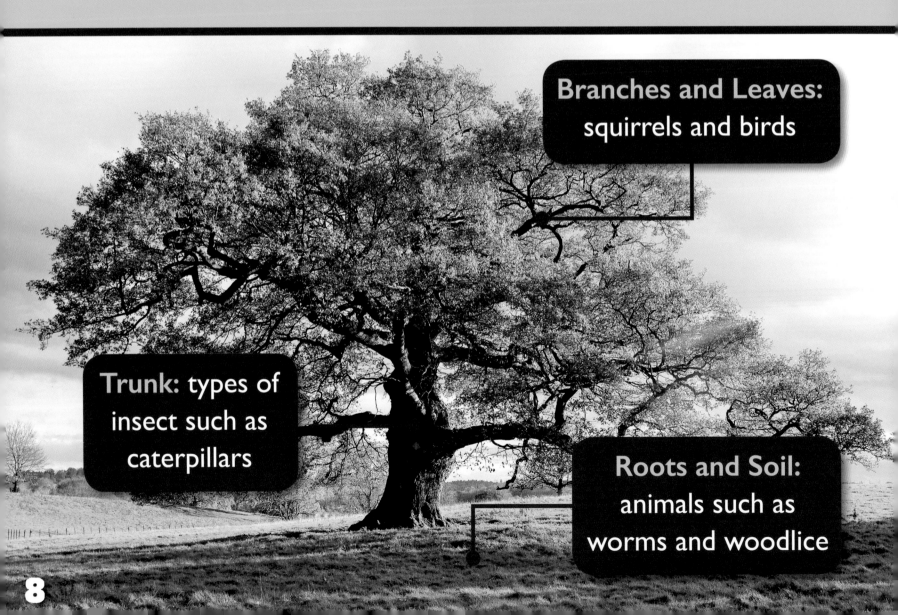

Branches and Leaves: squirrels and birds

Trunk: types of insect such as caterpillars

Roots and Soil: animals such as worms and woodlice

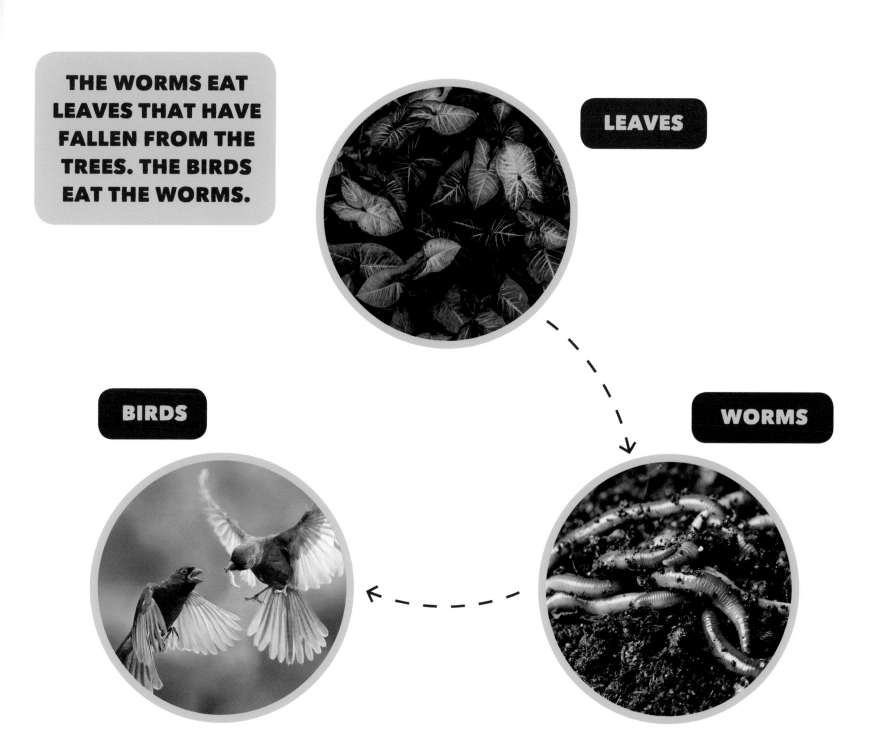

THE WORMS EAT LEAVES THAT HAVE FALLEN FROM THE TREES. THE BIRDS EAT THE WORMS.

LEAVES

BIRDS

WORMS

All the animals living in the same area need each other, and their habitat, to survive. Together, they make up an ecosystem.

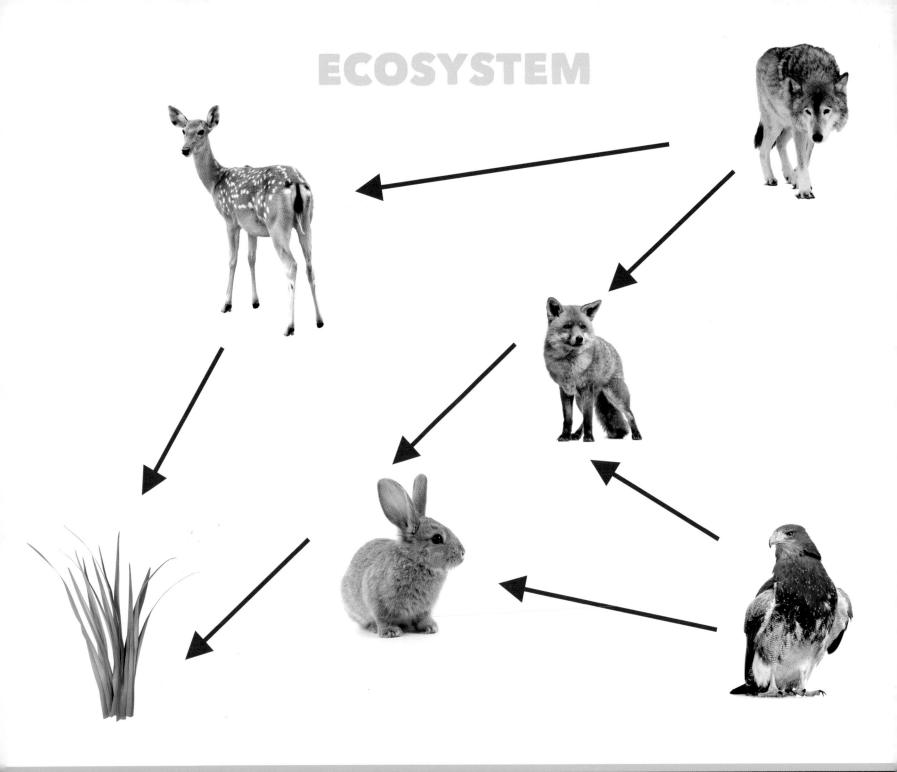

Every ecosystem in the world is linked. Together they form
a huge web of creatures and habitats.

When a habitat is damaged, or a species becomes endangered or extinct, it affects every other animal in the web. Conservation work tries to make sure that all ecosystems survive in the future.

IF PLANTS ARE DESTROYED, ANIMALS LIKE DEER AND RABBITS DO NOT HAVE ENOUGH FOOD TO SURVIVE. THIS CAN CAUSE PROBLEMS FOR PREDATORS, SUCH AS WOLVES AND BUZZARDS.

WHY ARE ANIMALS IN DANGER?

Animals are in danger partly as a result of **natural causes**. Many things can damage their habitats.

NATURAL CAUSES

FIRE

FLOOD

DISASTER

DISEASE

HUMAN ACTIVITY

OVERFISHING

POLLUTION

CLIMATE CHANGE

HUNTING

CUTTING DOWN TREES

Animals and their homes have mainly been put at risk because of things that humans have done.

BUILDING WORK INCREASES POLLUTION.

In recent times, there has been an **increase** in human **population** and so more space has been needed for building homes and growing food.

Conservation work can protect the habitats of many animals from human activity, **guaranteeing** the survival of their species.

WHICH ANIMALS
ARE AT RISK?

The IUCN have made a list which keeps track of species, their numbers and the reasons they are at risk.

THE IUCN STANDS FOR INTERNATIONAL UNION FOR THE CONSERVATION OF NATURE AND NATURAL RESOURCES.

IUCN

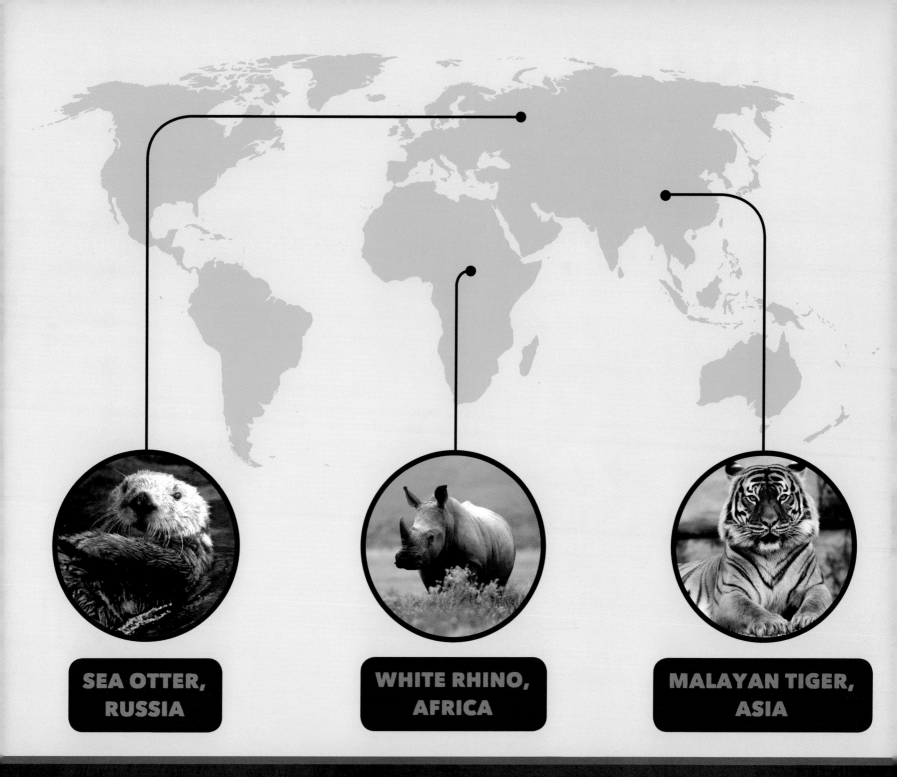

SEA OTTER, RUSSIA

WHITE RHINO, AFRICA

MALAYAN TIGER, ASIA

Animals from all around the world are at risk. It's important that we take care of the animals in our local area so as few animals as possible are put at risk.

CONSERVATION GROUPS

Conservation groups are groups of people who work together to help conserve animals and their habitats. There are lots of conservation groups all around the world.

They take action against things that happen which put animals at risk. Their actions might include **protests** or helping to tell others about conservation.

THE WWF

The World Wide Fund for Nature (WWF) is one of the largest conservation groups and has over five million **members** all around the world.

The WWF have helped to conserve habitats such as forests and oceans while also trying to reduce climate change.

HOW CAN
WE HELP?

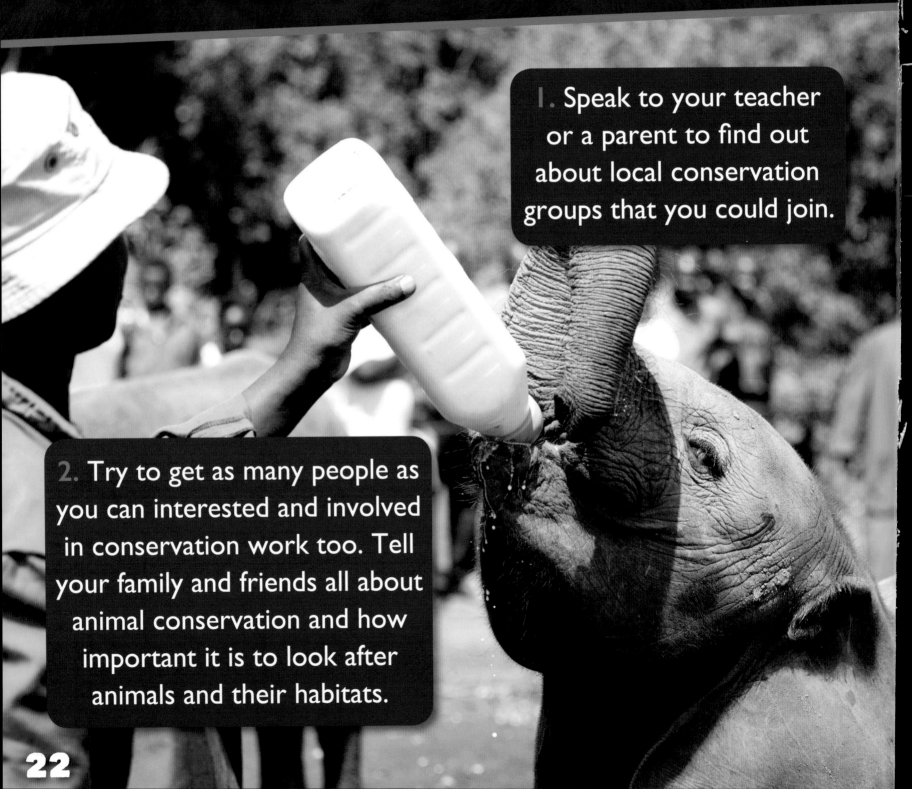

1. Speak to your teacher or a parent to find out about local conservation groups that you could join.

2. Try to get as many people as you can interested and involved in conservation work too. Tell your family and friends all about animal conservation and how important it is to look after animals and their habitats.

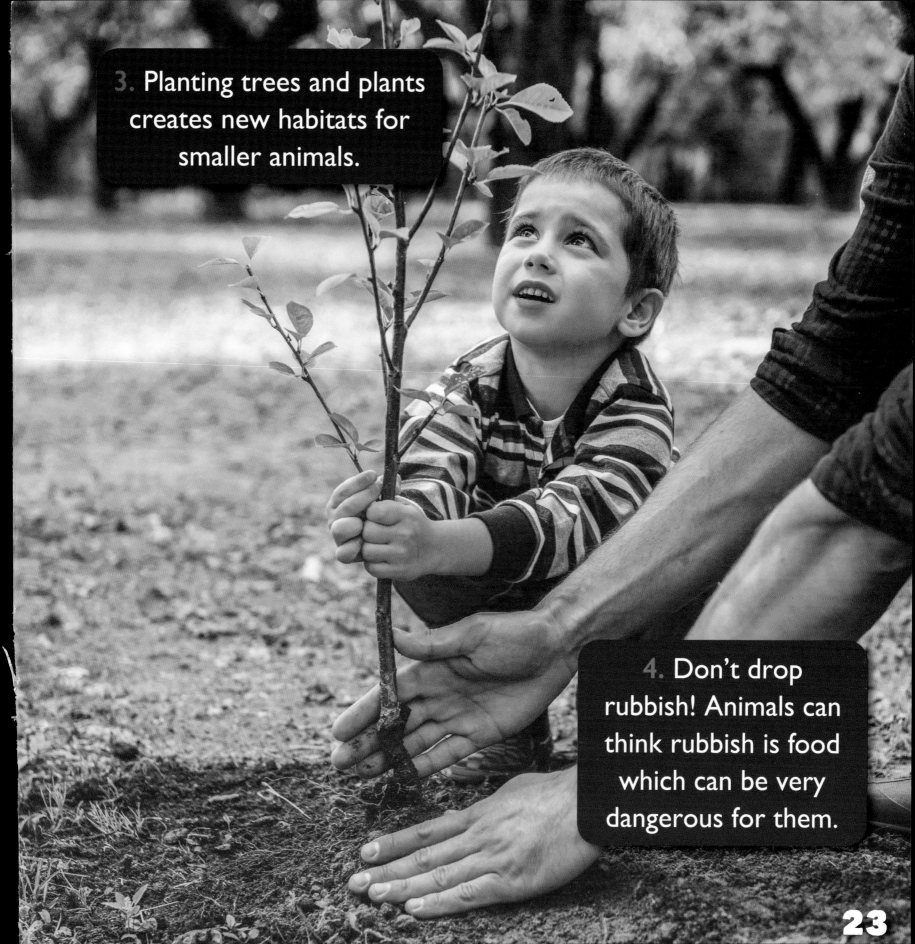

3. Planting trees and plants creates new habitats for smaller animals.

4. Don't drop rubbish! Animals can think rubbish is food which can be very dangerous for them.

23

GLOSSARY AND INDEX

GLOSSARY

climate change	long-term changes in the weather
destruction	causing so much damage to something that it no longer exists
guaranteeing	promising that a duty will be done
increase	becoming greater in size or amount
members	people belonging to a particular group
natural causes	things that happen because of nature
pollution	adding harmful or poisonous substances to the environment
population	the number of people living in a place
predators	animals that hunt other animals for food
protests	actively showing disapproval about something
species	a group of very similar animals or plants that are able to produce young together

INDEX